D0688649

TALL
NC
1478
.P86
H86
1985

Humorous Victorian
spot illustra-
tions

033101

DEC 1 88
APR 5 '89

Lake Tahoe Community College
Learning Resources Center
So. Lake Tahoe, CA 95702

Humorous Victorian Spot Illustrations

Edited by
Carol Belanger Grafton

DOVER PUBLICATIONS, INC.   NEW YORK

LAKE TAHOE COMMUNITY COLLEGE
LEARNING RESOURCES CENTER

033101

Copyright © 1985 by Dover Publications, Inc.
All rights reserved under Pan American and International Copyright Conventions.

Published in Canada by General Publishing Company, Ltd., 30 Lesmill Road, Don Mills, Toronto, Ontario.

Published in the United Kingdom by Constable and Company, Ltd., 10 Orange Street, London WC2H 7EG.

Humorous Victorian Spot Illustrations is a new work, first published by Dover Publications, Inc., in 1985.

DOVER *Pictorial Archive* SERIES

This book belongs to the Dover Pictorial Archive Series. You may use the designs and illustrations for graphics and crafts applications, free and without special permission, provided that you include no more than ten in the same publication or project. (For permission for additional use, please write to Dover Publications, Inc., 31 East 2nd Street, Mineola, N.Y. 11501.)

However, republication or reproduction of any illustration by any other graphic service whether it be in a book or in any other design resource is strictly prohibited.

Manufactured in the United States of America
Dover Publications, Inc., 31 East 2nd Street, Mineola, N.Y. 11501

Library of Congress Cataloging in Publication Data
Main entry under title:

Humorous Victorian spot illustrations.

(Dover pictorial archive series)
A selection of black and white spot illustrations originally appearing in Punch magazine from 1841-1914.
1. English wit and humor, Pictorial. 2. Great Britain—Social life and customs—19th century—Caricatures and cartoons. 3. Punch (London, England) I. Grafton, Carol Belanger. II. Series.
NC1478.P86H86 1985   741.5′942   85-4547
ISBN 0-486-24896-8 (pbk.)

Contents

Publisher's Note

First published in 1841, *Punch; or the London Charivari* has attained a position of international prominence that comes to few magazines. Liberal and rambunctious in its earlier years, by the 1860s it had settled down to a bourgeois viewpoint, reflecting the tastes and prejudices of the British middle class.

The magazine also gained favor in the 1860s for the high level of its artwork. Nineteenth-century contributors included John Tenniel, George du Maurier, Linley Sambourne, Phil May, Charles Keene and John Leech, to name but a few.

Carol Belanger Grafton has sifted through the thousands of illustrations that graced the pages of *Punch* from 1841 to 1914—the apogee of the British Empire—to produce the present volume. The selection is representative of the wide range of styles and subject matter that appeared in the magazine. Earlier works tended to be exaggerated and bizarre; later ones demonstrate greater technical polish and suavity. Sharp-eyed readers will recognize some familiar faces worked into the drawings: Lloyd George, Chamberlain, Bernhardt and, of course, Mr. Punch himself and his dog Toby. Similarly, there are references to matters that were of concern to *Punch*'s readership: the "new" woman; "huntin', fishin' and ridin'"; servants; class relations. None of these, however, needs concern the artist or designer who turns to the illustrations for a lively source of ideas or for direct use as pungent spot illustrations.

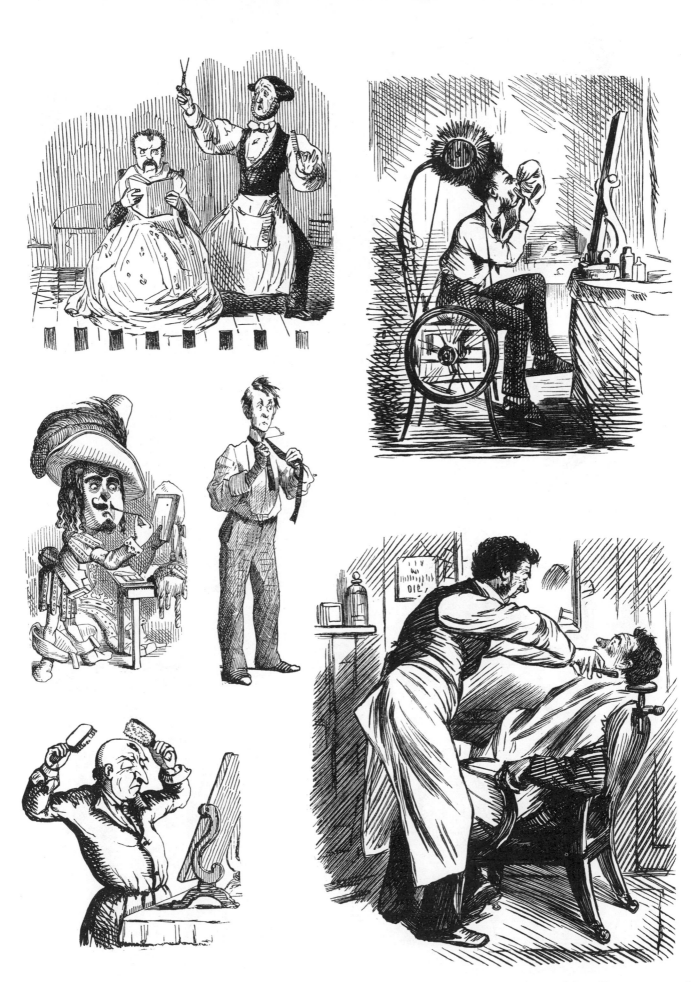

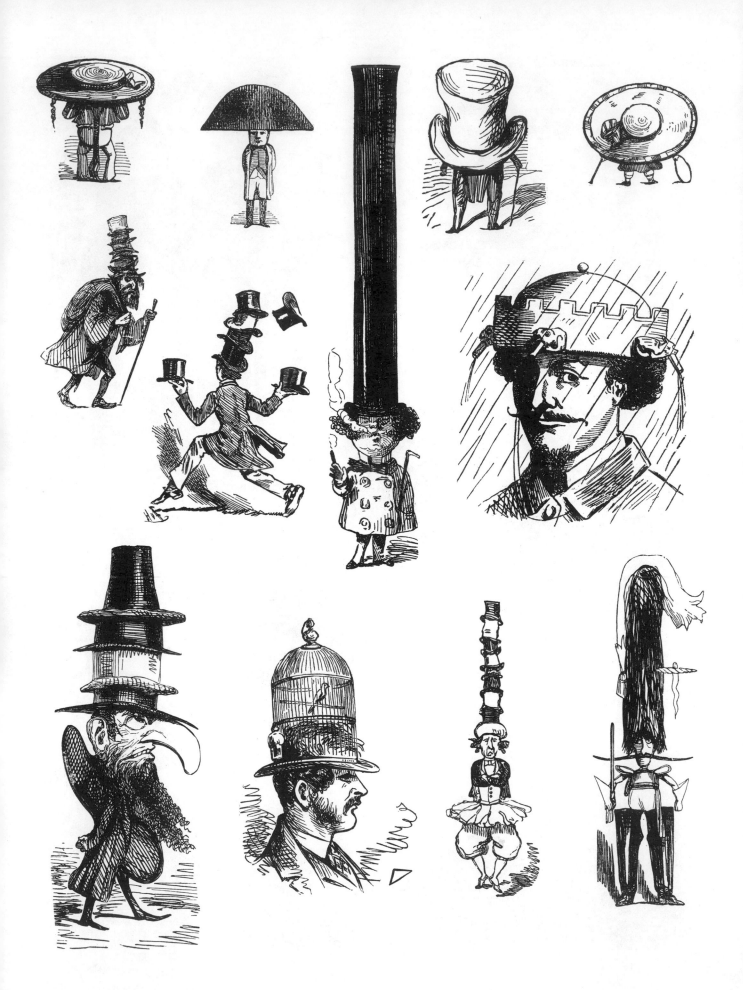

The text on the sign reads:

STROKE FOR WOMEN

NO STROKES FOR WOMEN

GIGANTIC DEMONSTRATION AT THE ALBERT HALL NOVEMBER 8 1911

THE NEW JOURNAL FOR GOLFING WOMANHOOD.

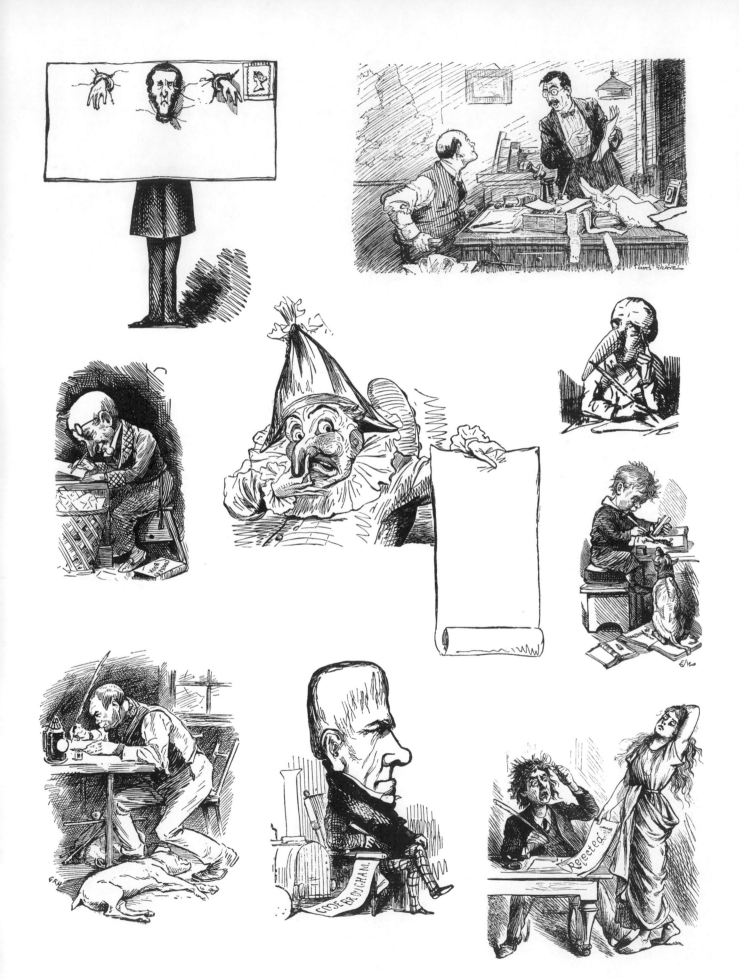

1909

9833